I0170802

A
Woman's
Worth

Inspirational Quotes for Women of
All Ages

CURT THOMAS

www.CurtThomasSpeaks.com

A Woman's Worth

ISBN: 978-0-9961977-0-0

Library of Congress Control Number: 2015904056

CURT THOMAS UNLIMITED, LLC Orangeburg, SC

www.CurtThomasSpeaks.com

Dedication

This book is dedicated to my first Queen, my loving mother. You were trusted to be a loving wife and to show my brother Bernard and I love from conception and to that, you have remained faithful!

Thank you mom...

...and to my lovely wife & "Twin Flame" Traci(Michael) and Andrea(Tyler and Preston), the mothers of my three beautiful sons Tyler, Preston, and Michael...

Thank you for my gifts...

...and to EVERY great grand mother, grandmother, mother, wife, daughter, sister, niece, grand-daughter around the world. You all are truly beautiful inside and out!

Thank you...

www.CurtThomasSpeaks.com

A Woman's Worth

A Woman's Worth

Quotes

www.CurtThomasSpeaks.com

A Woman's Worth

"*My mother believed in me before I wasn't mature enough to believe in myself.*"

~Curt Thomas

A Woman's Worth

"There is no such thing as an ugly woman."

~Vincent Van Gogh

"If a woman has to choose between catching a fly ball and saving an infant's life, she will choose to save the infant's life without even considering if there are men on base."

~Dave Barry

"*[W]omen are meant to be loved, not to be understood.*"

~Oscar Wilde

"You can do it Curt, just trust and believe God and everything will be alright."

~Lucille Thomas (Mother)

"Women like silent men. They think they're listening."

~Marcel Achard

"*Sure God created man before woman. But then you always make a rough draft before the final masterpiece.*"

~Author Unknown

A Woman's Worth

"While I know myself as a creation of God,

I am also obligated to realize and remember that

everyone else and everything else are also God's creation."

~Maya Angelou

"Every woman is beautiful until she speaks."

~Zimbabwean Proverb

"I am aware of my thoughts. I choose them carefully. There is nothing I can't be, do, or have. Where my mind goes my body will follow."

~Traci Thomas(Wife)

"*Women cannot complain about men anymore until they start getting better taste in them.*"

~Bill Maher

"Women are the real reason we get up every day. I'm talking about real men. If there were no women, I would not even have to bathe, because why would I care? These are guys I'm hanging with. I wake up for a woman every day of my life to make it happen for her."

~Steve Harvey

"*A male gynecologist is like an auto mechanic who has never owned a car.*"

~Carrie Snow

"*You start out happy that you have no hips or boobs. All of a sudden you get them, and it feels sloppy. Then just when you start liking them, they start drooping.*"

~*Cindy Crawford*

"*Every girl should use what Mother Nature gave her before Father Time takes it away.*"

~Laurence J. Peter

"The average woman would rather have beauty than brains, because the average man can see better than he can think."

~Author Unknown

"*A woman can say more in a sigh than a man can say in a sermon.*"

~Arnold Haultain

"Whatever women do they must do twice as well as men to be thought half as good. Luckily, this is not difficult."

~Charlotte Whitton

"Women are always beautiful."

~Ville Valo

"Don't wait around for other people to be happy for you. Any happiness you get you've got to make yourself."

~Alice Walker

"*The two women exchanged the kind of glance women use when no knife is handy.*"

~Ellery Queen

"Curve: The loveliest distance between two points."

~Mae West

"What would men be without women? Scarce, sir...mighty scarce."

~Mark Twain

"Children are the reward of life."

~African proverb

"Can you imagine a world without men? No crime and lots of happy fat women."

~Nicole Hollander

"*Women get the last word in every argument. Anything a man says after that is the beginning of a new argument.*"

~Author Unknown

"Next to the wound, what women make best is the bandage."

~Jules Barbey d'Aurevilly

"A pessimist is a man who thinks all women are bad. An optimist is a man who hopes they are."

~Chauncey Mitchell Depew

"*The rarest thing in the world is a woman who is pleased with photographs of herself.*"

~*Elizabeth Metcalf*

*"There is a special place
in hell for women who do
not help other women."*

~Madeleine K. Albright

"A man's face is his autobiography. A woman's face is her work of fiction."

~Oscar Wilde

A Woman's Worth

"There's something luxurious about having a girl light your cigarette. In fact, I got married once on account of that."

~Harold Robbins

"*My mother was the first Goddess I saw when I was born.*"

~Curt Thomas

"When a man talks dirty to a woman, it's sexual harassment. When a woman talks dirty to a man, it's $3.95 a minute."

~Author Unknown

"*Whether they give or refuse, it delights women just the same to have been asked.*"

~Ovid

A Woman's Worth

"However, I'm not denyin' the women are foolish: God Almighty made 'em to match the men."

~George Eliot

www.CurtThomasSpeaks.com

"Women really do rule
the world. They just
haven't figured it out yet.
When they do, and they
will, we're all in big big
trouble."

~Doctor Leon

"Ah, women. They make the highs higher and the lows more frequent."

~Friedrich Wilhelm Nietzsche

"*I expect Woman will be the last thing civilized by Man.*"

~George Meredith

"Men who don't like girls with brains don't like girls."

~Mignon McLaughlin

"Women keep a special corner of their hearts for sins they have never committed."

~Cornelia Otis Skinner

"*Lovely female shapes are terrible complicators of the difficulties and dangers of this earthly life, especially for their owners.*"

~George du Maurier

"*Every woman is wrong
until she cries, and then
she is right — instantly.*"

~*Sam Slick*

"*I have an idea that the phrase 'weaker sex' was coined by some woman to disarm some man she was preparing to overwhelm.*"

~Ogden Nash

"When men reach their sixties and retire, they go to pieces. Women go right on cooking."

~Gail Sheehy

"Trust yourself. Think for yourself. Act for yourself. Speak for yourself. Be yourself. Imitation is suicide."

~Marva Collins

"Be to her virtues very
kind,
Be to her faults a little
blind."

~Matthew Prior

"'I can't' are two words that have never been in my vocabulary. I believe in me more than anything in this world."

~Wilma Rudolph

"Think like a queen. A queen is not afraid to fail. Failure is another steppingstone to greatness."

~Oprah Winfrey

A Woman's Worth

"*They are no ugly women only lazy ones.*"

~*Traci Thomas*

"*You see, dear, it is not true that woman was made from man's rib; she was really made from his funny bone.*"

~J.M. Barrie

"If women didn't exist, all the money in the world would have no meaning."

~Aristotle Onassis

"*Men will always delight in a woman whose voice is lined with velvet.*"

~Brendan Francis

"Men really prefer reasonably attractive women; they go after the sensational ones to impress other men."

~Mignon McLaughlin

"Women dress alike all over the world: they dress to be annoying to other women."

~Elsa Schiaparelli

"*Women are never stronger than when they arm themselves with their weakness.*"

~*Marie de Vichy-Chamrond*

"If President Nixon's secretary, Rosemary Woods, had been Moses' secretary, there would only be eight commandments."

~Art Buchwald

"Woman begins by resisting a man's advances and ends by blocking his retreat."

~Oscar Wilde

"I'd much rather be a woman than a man. Women can cry, they can wear cute clothes, and they're the first to be rescued off sinking ships."

~Gilda Radner

"*She wore a short skirt and a tight sweater and her figure described a set of parabolas that could cause cardiac arrest in a yak.*"

~Woody Allen

"It is only rarely that one can see in a little boy the promise of a man, but one can almost always see in a little girl the threat of a woman."

~Alexandre Dumas

"But please don't cry, dry your eyes, never let up

Forgive but don't forget, girl keep your head up

And when he tells you you ain't nothin' don't believe him

And if he can't learn to love you you should leave him

Cause sista you don't need him."

~Tupac Shakur

"All women are basically in competition with each other for a handful of eligible men."

~Mignon McLaughlin

"*A woman should soften but not weaken a man.*"

~*Sigmund Freud*

"*Women are in league with each other, a secret conspiracy of hearts and pheromones.*"

~Camille Paglia

"When I glimpse the backs of women's knees I seem to hear the first movement of Beethoven's "Pastoral Symphony.""

~Author Unknown

"*A woman wears her tears like jewelry.*"

~*Author Unknown*

"*If a girl looks swell when she meets you, who gives a damn if she's late? Nobody.*"

~J.D. Salinger

"No woman wants to see herself too clearly."

~Mignon McLaughlin

"I prefer the word homemaker, because housewife always implies that there may be a wife someplace else."

~Bella Abzug

"*All that I am, or hope to be, I owe to my angel mother.*"

~Abraham Lincoln

"Women go to beauty
parlors for the unmussed
look men hate."

~Mignon McLaughlin

"There are women who do not like to cause suffering to many men at a time, and who prefer to concentrate on one man: These are the faithful women."

~Alfred Capus

"*A man sometimes wins an argument, but a woman always wins a silence.*"

~*Robert Brault*

"The girls that are always easy on the eyes are never easy on the heart."

~Author Unknown

A Woman's Worth

"*That strong mother doesn't tell her cub, Son, stay weak so the wolves can get you. She says, Toughen up, this is reality we are living in.*"

~Lauryn Hill

"*Judge not your beauty by the number of people who look at you, but rather by the number of people who smile at you.*"

~African Proverb

"*I've reached the age where competence is a turn-on.*"

~Billy Joel

"Being a lady is an attitude."

~*Chuck Woolery*

"*A man gives many question marks, however, a woman is a whole mystery.*"

~*Diana Stürm*

"God did it on purpose so that we may love you men instead of laughing at you."

~Mrs. Patrick Campbell

"Men at most differ as Heaven and Earth, but women, worst and best, as Heaven and Hell."

~Alfred Lord Tennyson

"*A woman asks little of love: only that she be able to feel like a heroine.*"

~Mignon McLaughlin

"The chief excitement in a woman's life is spotting women who are fatter than she is."

~Helen Rowland

"I would rather trust a woman's instinct than a man's reason."

~Stanley Baldwin

"I should like to know what is the proper function of women, if it is not to make reasons for husbands to stay at home, and still stronger reasons for bachelors to go out."

~George Eliot

"*Men look at themselves in mirrors. Women look for themselves.*"

~*Elissa Melamed*

"*If your husband expects you to laugh, do so; if he expects you to cry, don't; if you don't know what he expects, what are you doing married?*"

~Mignon McLaughlin

"Women do not find it difficult nowadays to behave like men, but they often find it extremely difficult to behave like gentlemen."

~Compton Mackenzie

"*One is not born a woman, one becomes one.*"

~Simone de Beauvoir

"Let us leave the
beautiful women to men
with no imagination."

~Marcel Proust

"Women deserve to have more than twelve years between the ages of twenty-eight and forty."

~James Thurber

"*The man's desire is for the woman; but the woman's desire is rarely other than for the desire of the man.*"

~*Samuel Taylor Coleridge*

"*After about twenty years of marriage, I'm finally starting to scratch the surface of that one. And I think the answer lies somewhere between conversation and chocolate.*"

~Mel Gibson

"Women who make men talk better than they are accustomed to are always popular."

~E. V. Lucas

"*A man is as good as he has to be, and a woman is as bad as she dares.*"

~Elbert Hubbard

"*You should never say anything to a woman that even remotely suggests that you think she's pregnant unless you can see an actual baby emerging from her at that moment.*"

~*Dave Barry*

"*The supply of good women far exceeds that of the men who deserve them.*"

~*Robert Graves*

"*A woman should be an illusion.*"

~*Ian Fleming*

"There are three things men can do with women: love them, suffer for them, or turn them into literature."

~Stephen Stills

"*It is because of men that women dislike one another.*"

~*Jean de La Bruyère*

"Look like a girl, act like a lady, think like a man and work like a dog."

~Caroline K. Simon

"If you are ever in doubt as to whether to kiss a pretty girl, always give her the benefit of the doubt."

~Thomas Carlyle

"*Women who feel naked without their lipstick are well over thirty.*"

~*Mignon McLaughlin*

"It's simple. Women only nag when they feel unappreciated."

~Louis de Bernières

"It's the good girls who keep the diaries; the bad girls never have the time."

~Tallulah Bankhead

"*I think God made a woman to be strong and not to be trampled under the feet of men. I've always felt this way because my mother was a very strong woman, without a husband.*"

~Little Richard

"*A husband only worries about a particular other Man; a wife distrusts her whole species.*"

~Mignon McLaughlin

"*A woman who cannot be ugly is not beautiful.*"

~*Karl Kraus*

"*A man chases a woman until she catches him.*"

~*American Proverb*

"Beauty is the first present nature gives to women, and the first it takes away."

~Méré

"There's just something about letting a girl have her way with you."

~A.C. Van Cherub

"Usually the woman has an appointment with destiny, and the man just happens to be there."

~Robert Brault

"Once a woman has given you her heart, you can never get rid of the rest of her."

~John Vanbrugh

"*Is it too much to ask that women be spared the daily struggle for superhuman beauty in order to offer it to the caresses of a subhumanly ugly mate?*"

~Germaine Greer

"A beautiful thing is never perfect."

~Egyptian Proverb

"*Do you not know I am a woman? when I think, I must speak.*"

~William Shakespeare

"*Women are wiser than men because they know less and understand more.*"

~James Thurber

"Good-looking girls break hearts, and goodhearted girls mend them."

~Mignon McLaughlin

"Fighting is essentially a masculine idea; a woman's weapon is her tongue."

~Hermione Gingold

A Woman's Worth

"Biology is the least of what makes someone a mother."

~Oprah Winfrey

"Women always worry about the things that men forget; men always worry about the things women remember."

~Author Unknown

"*No matter how happily a woman may be married, it always pleases her to discover that there is a nice man who wishes that she were not.*"

~H.L. Mencken

"*I am a flawed man, but I'm grateful to have been blessed to have three wonderful sons with flawless spirts! For that I am forever grateful to the wounds who bore them.*"

~Curt Thomas

A Woman's Worth

~Thank you...

Curt

A Woman's Worth

A Woman's Worth

Like us on Facebook:

Keyword: Curt Thomas Motivational Speaker

Instagram:

Keyword: @CurtThomasSpeaks

Follow on Twitter:

Keyword: @CurtSpeaks